Praise for *Irregular Heart*

"An elegiac collection of close calls—in which the velvet rope and the dead, the past and the present, permits easy passage—Russell Brakefield's sonorously delicious *Irregular Heartbeats at the Park West* proclaims that 'The sharper edge of nostalgia is knowing you barely got out alive.' Brakefield wipes his 'hand across death's edge' not just to illustrate some lamentation on loss but as a way to show how to celebrate it: 'Give me the dead / tonight, troves / of them / clambering / up from the dirt.' Souls on both sides of the celestial divide party and get down together in these pages. Boy, am I grateful for the invitation."

—Tommye Blount, author of *Fantasia for the Man in Blue*

"'What's the half-life of trauma?' It's a fitting question for a book which tenderly, thoughtfully explores how much our present selves are constituted by the haunting of our pasts, as well as the constant threat of our own mortality. Russell Brakefield is a poet we can trust with our existential fears."

—Nicky Beer, author of *Real Phonies and Genuine Fakes*

"'There, in the world,' writes Brakefield, 'was the language for everything.' And the language with which Brakefield brings that world to us is piercingly inventive. *Irregular Heartbeats at the Park West* is a striking collection by a writer of considerable skill."

—Matthew Olzmann, author of *Constellation Route*

Praise for *Field Recordings*

"Brakefield beautifully inscribes how one internalizes the ephemeral nature of home."

—*Rain Taxi*

"It is fascinating to see a young poet staking his claim forcefully and beautifully in his first book."

—*Ann Arbor Observer*

"With folk music as his guide, Brakefield traverses the Great Lakes region in these poems, from its primordial beginning to its modern days. 'In the beginning all art was audible,' he writes in a collection that ambles through the natural world while keeping a finger firmly on the pulse of how the world shapes people into what they are. At its center is one poem: a long-form, multi-stanza piece inspired by oral historian Alan Lomax, who, in 1938, traveled around the Great Lakes basin, collecting recordings. This titular poem has elements of Whitman's 'Crossing Brooklyn Ferry' in its dreamy scope and its traversing of time and space. But the rest of the collection roams widely as well, touching on ideas of family and masculinity ('This is America and we are boys / slowly tiring into our fathers') and on how people so often cannot be still ('Movement of people / or animals across land is called migration / and also displacement'). Deeply rooted in its oral histories, Brakefield's collection sings."

—*Booklist*

"Firmly rooted in the dramatic landscapes and histories of Michigan, *Field Recordings* uses American folk music as a lens to investigate themes of personal origin, family, art, and masculinity. The speakers of these poems navigate Michigan's folklore and folkways while exploring more personal connections to those landscapes and examining the timeless questions that occupy those songs and stories. With rich musicality and lyric precision, the poems in *Field Recordings* look squarely at what it means to be a son, a brother, an artist, a person."

—*New Pages*

"Brakefield says a man can't be 'anything that doesn't / move for fear / of standing still' and all sound, all music, is motion, the cure for stillness. But these poems occupy both states equally: the ways we craft sound and story to crowd out silence and fear, and the stillness that precipitates but also defines whatever music we can manage. Here, the necessary paradox is sweet and stark, carefully tuned to its places of origin, and the people—here and gone—whose echoes haunt them."

—Raymond McDaniel, author of *The Cataracts*

"Like the great Alan Lomax, Russell Brakefield has traveled through rural Michigan making 'field recordings.' He listens to the music and to the instruments that make the music (the double bass 'gathers up grace'—which seems the perfect description of those notes!). And he talks to the people who make the music and then listen to it. These poems don't forget the shores and the birch trees, the sea birds or the 'clumsy pub.' He tells us that in 'this Peninsula I'm no more minstrel than ghost, / minor chord, blue note.' I don't think Russell Brakefield's chords, his poems, are minor at all; they are strong and clear and make the necessary music."

—Keith Taylor, author of *The Bird-while* (Wayne State University Press)

"Russell Brakefield is that rare, best kind of poet whose insights can change the world for his readers, who unveils the wild surprises and lurking dangers behind the seemingly familiar. Beneath his 'buildings falling into pieces' there is the 'rapture of foundations, / a storm of rust // and bodies raining up / against the sky.' The world becomes clearer, stranger, and more uncanny as we read this poetry. Brakefield astonishes again and again in *Field Recordings*—a book full of individually riveting pieces, but one which, as a whole, casts a serious spell with its accumulating music and beauty and everyday sacredness, with its sacred, ordinary horror and wonder. Brakefield has written one of the strongest and most subtle collections of poetry I've read in a long time. This is a collection to which one will return again and again, becoming ever more impacted by its power and more appreciative of the serious talent of this poet."

—Laura Kasischke, author of *Where Now: New and Selected Poems*

IRREGULAR HEARTBEATS
AT THE PARK WEST

Made in Michigan Writers Series

GENERAL EDITORS

Michael Delp, Interlochen Center for the Arts
M. L. Liebler, Wayne State University

A complete listing of the books in this series can
be found online at wsupress.wayne.edu.

Irregular Heartbeats at the Park West

POEMS

by Russell Brakefield

WAYNE STATE UNIVERSITY PRESS
DETROIT

ISBN 9780814351024 (paperback)
ISBN 9780814351031 (e-book)

Library of Congress Control Number: 2023939005

Cover design by Brad Norr Design.

Excerpt from "A Primer" by Bob Hicok, from *Words for Empty, Words for Full* (University of Pittsburgh Press, 2010). Reprinted by permission of Bob Hicok.

Publication of this book was made possible by a generous gift from The Meijer Foundation.

Wayne State University Press rests on Waawiyaataanong, also referred to as Detroit, the ancestral and contemporary homeland of the Three Fires Confederacy. These sovereign lands were granted by the Ojibwe, Odawa, Potawatomi, and Wyandot Nations, in 1807, through the Treaty of Detroit. Wayne State University Press affirms Indigenous sovereignty and honors all tribes with a connection to Detroit. With our Native neighbors, the press works to advance educational equity and promote a better future for the earth and all people.

Wayne State University Press
Leonard N. Simons Building
4809 Woodward Avenue
Detroit, Michigan 48201-1309

Visit us online at wsupress.wayne.edu.

CONTENTS

I.

II.

I.

Let us all be from somewhere.
Let us tell each other everything we can.

—Bob Hicok

Prayers for Home (i)

The old rope swing still sways like a noose
        to the moon's face.
The creek bed below cradles my body, wraps me
in a lock of broken glass and tangled test.
        Lampreys troll the depths, feed on ghosts—
my teenage self, the friend once swept under
and reborn downstream, bloated and stiff
        by the boat docks. In the trees,
ghost boys run wild with juice in their teeth.
They gather on riverbanks and practice standing
        like grown men above the quarries.
I've inked the veins of the whole county tonight,
beamed a headlight page on the road
        and written nothing good.
Prayer, as I know it, is slow to work. It slinks
to the surface of the body like sweat. But still,
        I offer devotions tonight
to the mayfly, to the deer eyes firing
through red alders, to the muddy wash below.
        There is dark magic here, dark magic
in the places we only find ourselves lost.

Family History

Cartons of curled photographs.
Stacked boxes binding the bones
of my ancestors. Chipped china
swept off a farmhouse floor.
A hinged heart carried over
sea and meadow, folded into
a kerchief from the old country.
Maybe someday I'll find this
catalog of evidence, this record
of how my family lived and died.
But then, maybe not. Maybe
the silence in the house was
not just Midwestern kindness
but something else, the kitchen
always buzzing with present tense—
boiling pot, sweating kettle,
dishes stacking in the sink.
We measured trauma in teacups,
doused with heavy cream.
Survival, mutters my grandmother
from her armchair, from deep inside
a dementia fog. She raises her hand
in grade school. She assembles
metal casters on a factory line.
Her mind skips again and she is
being chased across the tundra,
held at gunpoint in a foreign land.
Survival, she whispers and means
it is a burden to carry
all our histories within us.

Junk

In the old neighborhood, a boy drinks color with his eyes.
    A boy sucks music through the straws in his arms.

Local news, muted at the sports bar: "EMS Battles Lethal Cocktail."
    One metaphor carts off another, as though enough

language could lift away the bodies for good. My hometown
    scrolls the screen like a single victim, a eulogy

ticker taping monitors above the barroom clatter.
    The sharper edge of nostalgia is knowing you barely got out alive.

Time turns low the house lights, and the TVs turn to football,
    and I'm dragged to the scene of a house fire,

windows full of smoke and ash, windows full
    of different versions of myself.

Pyromaniac

On the porch, my father
wears his workday out
in the open. He's telling
the sitter about the fires,
about my recent interest
in spectacle, in ruin.
But I thought we'd agreed
not to say. That I'd be his
tiny madman and he my
silent partner. That each
collapse I forged would
be partly his to claim.

Work

Some days the work hums loud enough
        to play a sweet song at my temple—
a topcoat of treble, tremble of bass
        from the belt sander or nail gun.
But then Lee remembers he's forgotten
        the boom box, and it's back
to endless hours of The Eagles,
        Foghat, Journey, repeat.
And what does it really matter?
        All those fathers that warned us
you become what you let in
        are dead or dying anyway.
We are all left to build the house alone.
        Next to me, Lee trembles behind
the nail gun, the punch of each pin
        rippling up his forearm
like a brushstroke on a living canvas.
        In each tack, a portrait taking shape.
In the heat and beneath the shriek of Styx,
        I push a bit of sawdust on my brow
to stop the sweat—an offering, a gospel,
        a prayer of thanks
to my hands and back, which will go
        as everything, at last, does.
For the sun and my shadow, a crumpled
        dial keeping time on the pavement.
At night when I peel off my jeans,
        they hold the shape of my legs
and lean to the floor like an old man
        kneeling in prayer.

Repetitive Motion

"And ghosts must do again what gives them pain."

—W. H. Auden

Like the seamstress who dreams in darning stitch.

The carpenter who swings his hammer from the grave.

Or spirit hands above an assembly line,
  swimming endless circles on the factory floor.

*   *   *

What does this mean for my mother,
  who answered phones for years at the women's shelter
    downtown
  to listen and listen and listen for the sound of breathing?

How to Cast a Fly

i.

Let your arm ride the horizon
                like a day moon
         cut in a clean quarter

tug the current like a silk
                scarf from a crystal
        work the tremble—

pyrite and minnow—
                of the Ouija's arrow
        the weight

of life swelling
                electric gold and blue
        wind in the ground

gilled kites caught there
                with the beat stones
        and burrowing shells

ii.

despite the saying
                I step back often
        into the same moving water

the Chippewa River
                boxes of caught sunlight
        littering the banks

could this be
                the one mystic pulse
        beneath everything else

that life must be lived over
                          and over
            killdeer back in spring

steelhead tied
                          to the winter run
            turning downstream to spawn

then turning back again
                          and again to some deep
            embedded origin

Cliff Jumpers at the Dead River Gorge

When we found him
on the path, the boy

cradled on his head
a ripe wound. He turned

to retch into the reeds,
a school of minnows

swarming his bloody
crown. We watched

him drift the stream bed,
his limbs forming

the current's shadow,
watched him expel trouble

in sharp spasms near
his mouth and brow,

the frailty of our form
unfolding before us

like a floating white lily.
And after, the other boys

circled like wolves
around a dead wolf,

unwilling to leave
the pile of fur and bones

should some final howl
break loose. A cry

from beyond. A warning
or perhaps a curse.

The Fiberglass Man

Janitor by Duane Hanson, Milwaukee Museum of Art

i.

As with a hitch or limp
                    he steps from his mark
        his uniform worn in
at the natural spots

elbows and pockets blanched
                   keychain like a hive at his hip
        we wait for him to move
to break his labored stance

we are undone by his resemblance
                   the mirror maker's timeless trick
        by the way he fades
from the gallery, erased

by his olive blouse
                   by the corona
        of stinky bodies around him
we are undone

by his posture, his body
                   bent low as if being called back
        and back again—like us—
to the greedy earth

ii.

Everyone else has moved on
                   to the reliquaries, the Cornell in the corner
        Celestial Navigation by Birds
five goblets holding nothing

but he and I are locked here together
                    he and I and, suddenly, my mother
          who for years worked night shifts
at the middle school

wheeled a cart and bucket
                    trays of blue and yellow solvents
          her own clutch of keys
swinging like a hive at her hip

me and the janitor
                    and the docents in matching vests
          and my mother, here twenty years later,
squeaking her rubber shoes

on the gallery floors
                    my young mother
          fading into the background
in a dozen different shirts

with a dozen different tags
                    each whispering her name
          in stitched cursive
just above her heart

The Herman Melville House

"And wrecks passed without sound of bells."
                    —Hart Crane, "At Melville's Tomb"

How quickly he cut to his prepared remarks,
the tour guide in his period garb. How quickly
he cut to the specifics of the house—oil lamps
and black scars on the wallpaper, whale oil
spark for the old master to write, Mt. Greylock's
hump breaching the window box. How quickly
he cut past that bit about the wife and kids.
Like the skip of a fiddler's bow—tremble, scratch,
then on to the simpler music of the study, the loo,
rope bunks in the bedroom. How quickly he cut
past the rest and left more than one of us
back in the kitchen with our own modest pasts—
my own maternal line flattened beneath a storm
of heavy fists—which will not be canonized
and not, thank God, be opened to the public,
which will dim like the black wicks lining the walls,
burnt inside their glass urns. In the gift shop
two crones quarreled the cost of a bumper sticker
that read "Ignorance is the parent of fear." But what part
of fear is silence? And where are the children now?
And how hungry the whale we still refuse to kill?

Stop-Motion with Sunken Carcass

The deer were dying before I left, farm roads burned
in elegant blacktop, my father's rows of steak tomatoes

hanging like relics in the yard. The neighborhood's hiding spots—
shadowy and child shaped—already swept away or covered up

by commerce, the brewery and new hotel, drive-throughs
on big-box row. And I heard the boy down the street—

a man now but still living home and still scarred
from the Roman candle that streaked his ear when we were young—

overdosed in his garage just yesterday,
there with the bikes and ski gear and rusted mowers.

Should I feel lucky to have traced the line back here
to the first one to inject violence into my life?

I'll pretend the news means nothing, that his hands don't
still fold like purple flowers on my skin. He looked better

with the scar, even years later, in his ratty white T-shirts,
hot starting his old man's Indian in the driveway. Smoke in his lips

like a tunnel to the darkest edges of my life. Now all I can see
is his body laid out, still ropey and muscular but undone

inside black veins. A snap of pleasure imagining
his chalky corpse. How you might watch with wonder

a stop-motion video of a sunken carcass—a spring doe's body
percolating on the roadside—and not think at all

of the incredible precision of each mite picking flesh,
bacteria wilting her spots, maggots melting

her shoulders and cheeks gracefully down to bone.
What's the half-life of trauma? If you look closely, you'll see

me there in the weeds today, down where we used to ditch
our bikes over the guardrail. That's me, naked and feral,

tearing the doe from her cradle, crawling through the same
trash and gravel and grass, the nest I can't stop coming back to.

Too Lean on Joy to Be the Dog

Spring bloomed roadkill on the shoulders for years,
ghost deer bounding from muddy fields.

                              And when vultures came
to feed, I could not turn away from my open windows.
                              I could not stop drooling.

Find me in the old photos licking my chops,
grinding a hungry blood tooth.

                              Were you once too?
Too lean on joy to be the dog,
you lived in the body of the wolf instead.

My Mother's Hands

If I am allergic to honeybees (I am),
                then my mother is
a vibrant primrose, drawing life
                from the stingers that settle
in her palms and fingertips.
                She nuzzles blue azaleas, huffs
bee balm and hocks
                like each stem were an oxygen mask.
See what we call resilience
                in her almost every move—
afternoons she sweeps sleepy bees
                from the sills
as if cupping her hand in a well to drink.
                I wish someone would call me
resilient, just so I could show them
                my mother's hands,
twining mint in bunches or twisting
                the hot lid of a jam jar.
I should hold tight
                the twinning strands of DNA
between us. But here's the truth:
                in the midnight garden,
I'm tended like the olive tree, feeble
                but exalted, and she like the snake plant
or the pineapple, alive in a world
                adamant to break her open.

Jack Kerouac's Grave

And though, with context, I might've figured
what a "fuckboy" was,

my students delighted in having to tell me—

    Sal is a fuckboy and Dean should be canceled—

and we spent two weeks untangling questions
about gender and language I had not considered.

In the back, Melanie raises her hand:

    how lonely to be a woman in this book

she says, and then

    how lonely too to be a man.

Office Hours

There's an app now to remind you, twice daily, you will die.
As in a dream or a midnight movie, the doomsday clock rolls forward

in our pockets. In the news, gunshots report and report
like a Greek chorus. Shell casings fall into my cuffs and shirt pockets.

In my office, I'm stuck mid-sentence telling a student how
music hijacks the brain, how consonants create an alternate current

on the tongue, an alternate shore and sea, an alternate sun.
A sudden trembling then—a fat robin thrashing in panic

in the sunken window box behind us. The student flinches.
The room echoes the sound of students flinching.

The robin thumps its beak, first an unsteady tempo and then
an immeasurable silence. *What type of meter is that?* they ask

almost daily, and what I tell them is not unlike birdsong
placed tenderly in a poem about dying.

Flight Plans

I tell my students about the dodo
                 and the passenger pigeon
       but they don't believe me

that such animals could exist
                 or that beauty will ever be
       that at odds with abundance

when I'm with you
                 I become obsessed
       with the unwelcome mutations

occurring inside your body
                 duplication of one bent cell
       to another to another to another . . .

but on your scarf tonight
                 intricate birds
       crane their necks in flight

a confetti of contours
                 and on your dress, the same
       a canvas of blue birds

singing in chorus
                 against the uncertain world
       and your laugh follows

a perfect flight plan all its own
                 perfect product of biology
       portent only

for all the good left to come
                 your throat full of feathers
       the color of a cloudless sky

Prayers for Home (ii)

Sometime after I left,
the nature of the metaphor
broke. What once was
hook and cleaver dulled.
What once was blood pan
and collar turned to rust.
The bait shop windows
spilled a tongue of glass
in the alley. I still dream, to
this day, of chickens
in their crooked stalls,
stockyard rows beside
the highway, drainage tubes
where we fucked and smoked,
where we prayed prayers
of ascension. Now, an old friend
tells me, a Walmart. Pools
and sidewalks. Manicured lawns.
All the undead tweakers
sold out and the farmers too.
What's left, I wonder,
of what's made me
broken a little, yoked
to a certain type of sadness.
In my chest today a stone
rolls off. The sun breaks
by the levy where I'm still
a boy tearing the legs
from frogs and casting
their bodies like softballs
across the field and toward
a different life out beyond.

James Tate's Bookshelf

How does the tiger feel about his needle teeth?
And how about his stripes? He stalks

at twilight between the dusty hardcovers.
What tooth-shaped piece of me is missing

that I would steal this snarling, plastic figurine?
That I can't face the after party—tea candles

in the yard, cloves and small talk, white tablecloths,
an old-fashioned weeping in my fist? No ideas

but in things, and the hunter in my pocket
brings me closer, I suppose, to an idea of myself

I can stand. In the living room, I run
my fingers down its back and think what power

it might bring me. The power to birth
a menagerie, word by word,

and spiral each species until the world is
reflected—the flaws and tricks, drool

dripping down the jowls, stomach flayed
open and everything there exposed.

Astonishing, what we will do
to be the maker and not the made,

what we will tell ourselves about ourselves
to feel alive. A poem I read years ago

comes back to me in a flash—*a tiger
has the same number of bones in it as a monkey*—

long lines stalking me in the open grass.
My poems are like stones, by contrast,

dropped to the bottom of a clear pond,
the water's surface left untouched.

False Morels

as an act of mercy
as many lessons at once

he led us as boys
to an order of mushrooms

spared by his mower's blade
their squat heads

braided in brown spirals
a flock of friars gathered

beneath the elm tree
danger is so coded

in the wilder kingdom—
each color either

a funeral veil
or a Janus mask

and what we have gained
in history

we have lost in instinct
our boyhands

stingy for the tawny blooms
hovering there

in the yard
to cut them, he said

would force the spread
and even then

I felt how laughable
our attempts at dominion

opened up
thick webs ran through

the cap and stem
brain-like folds

clouding the cavity
saying *I am an enemy*

unmask me
I am a reminder

how close you are
to dust

Oysters

shell cradled like Poseidon's

rough palm in my own

a reminder of the primordial

we hook arms and suck

salt barely touching our tongues

and I sink back to the docks

and train tracks

and back lots of my childhood

knives across our thumbs

to bind us together

I will drink it in, this brotherhood

held up for a moment

tipped back on these ancient rafts

the world spins on for eons

our time here

as small as a washed pearl

Shadow Ball Haibun

April 2020

The boys laced under cover of night and ran the bases, or rather, ran to where the bases had once been. They floated over scars on the infield, phones glowing like shadow balls at the corners. They hollered out to ghosts, felt the winds of history running through them. *No field should be so quiet*, said one boy. *No pitch should be so empty*. A half-moon lifted a crooked spotlight. The wet grass painted their knees. One boy stepped into the batter's box. One boy cupped his hands and coughed up chants of a crowd, which mixed with the city noise, distant sirens, the night traffic on Trumbull. In the weeds, where the dugout had been, one boy ran his hands across his face, touched his lips and chin, called sign after sign from an invented playbook.

> in my notes today
> I write down the phrase *plague book*
> again by mistake

Personal Protective Equipment

Darwin knew for certain
other primates also wept.
On YouTube I watch,

on repeat, a lemur
send low, human howls
into the trees

trees from where his mate
has just been snatched.
A million songs

are written every minute
by predators'
gnashing teeth

by the intricate dance
of blowflies in soft tissue.
In other words

I'm thinking of Meagan's voice
on the phone today
as she counted aloud

the patients she's lost.
What do I do
with this sound?

Where does music go
in the brain
when it's not music at all

but the tempo
of the dead
walking on without us?

My Father's Breathing

Bees the color of sunset
sing in the aspen groves,

yellow fingers snapping
in the aspen groves and I listen

for these more natural sounds.
Behind me on the path,

the natural sound
of my father's breathing breaks

like an old song sung again
by an old singer,

a song we remember
but in a different tenor.

Or perhaps dying
has just the one tone

and every day we merely
wrap our ear in a new horn.

His breath shallows in my ears.
At the meadow, he sinks

into a field of Russian sage.
He actually reclines,

like a child, in the rash
of purple stems,

and is inflated
by the kitchen smell, a finch's

shuffle, field of bees
the color of the setting sun.

Relic

years from now I dislodge a mask

kneeling in a gas station parking lot

to suck crumbs from the consoles

half in and half out the passenger seat

I dislodge a mask from the floor mat

flattened and streaked, folded on itself

like a wounded bird but still

reattaining its feather-blue tint

ear straps flung aside like broken wings

its sunken breast smudged

where I once pressed my mouth

the downy screen through which

I filtered my life, where my words were

wrung out and carried off as on a soft wind

a dirty plume that held prayers

and songs and desperate transactions

where I said even, *I love you*

in a muffled tone, where I said even

I'm home! standing in the doorway

forgetting, for just a moment, which

were the safer parts of the world

II.

Come song,
allow me some eloquence,
good people die.

–Jim Harrison

Irregular Heartbeats at the Park West

Chicago

What started as a nest of bodies,
humming harmony in blue stage light,
unravels to neon and mist. My limbs
answer to each note like a puppet—
a buzz running throat to dance floor,
slick guitar solo opening my chest,
funk of weed and sweat, thunder
thud of bass drum cruising my system.
Earlier, the doctor's own tiny speaker
probed for a more regular beat.
A murmur, he said, indistinct whole note
bursting the otherwise dulcet
chorus of the body. On the phone,
when I told my father, he said
Well yes, me too. Like a confession,
a misplayed cymbal, a simple dip
in rhythm. At set break, it's the same
old talk—who's quit drinking
and who's checked in. More shows
means a longer list of losses,
a litany under the glow of house lights.
And no one even dares mention
the dead. Set two, the venue swells
like a ripe vein—empty beer cans
clogging the lanes at my feet,
the balcony's shadowy vessels.
Irregular doesn't always mean abnormal,
the doctor had said and warmed
his stethoscope again. But buried
in the pit, I pray for a stranger
to pass spoon or spliff, for the band
to play on and play on forever,

the crowd to swell and consume me,
to crush me into a fine dust.
No one really wants to be clairvoyant.
For what would account for all this?
Throttle of bass, minor chords
blooming on my sternum, the way
we keep on living like there's more
than one human outcome.

After Party

the afterlife

      shadows of the greenroom

      same sad song on the stereo

we all seek our saviors somewhere—

      empty chest

      of domestic beer

      a crowded bathroom stall

like faithful sentinels staying on in this

      bunker   backroom

      balcony   trailer

to lap up what's left of the night

      the saddle of regret

      cinching at the edges

even our parents knew   finally

      that music is only anatomical

      a bloodbeat against the skin

like everything else   of the body

      both balm and bruise

      a sinking boat   the ice

melting in a highball

Arcade

for Jess

It could be anything that sticks but happens with me
            to be a redemption game.
That is to say, I'm losing at Skee-ball
every time I think of you.

Every time I think of you
you are wrapped in a circus march.
Above us burns a row of translucent bulbs,
            filaments asking—I know now—
if I want this to be one of the few memories I'll have left
            to return to when you're gone.

My mouth, in the aftermath, fills with pinballs.
My chest clatters in the mornings like a struck paddle, a sprocket
            sprung by some hidden hammer.

As a dream slides off today, I fall into another and another—
I'm a dirty quarter clicking a slot, a nest of wires, split
            and poorly wrapped.

Even with loss, we keep our tallies—one week gone,
then the next. One life, then the next.

I once heard a story of a man who, in his grief, fell in love
            with his *Pac-Man*.
In the basement, he held his body close.
He bent by the crackling screen to warm his face,
            red and blue buttons like knuckles in his mouth.

Mourning, it turns out, is its own
            simulation—the screen black and blinking,
the path narrow and savage and ghosted.

Postscript for Jess

Grief does shrewd business,
wields ingenious tools to keep us close—

snapshots and melodies, memory
a cruel accomplice. My anger is

at its worst today, when the song
that brings you back is the *Galaga* theme

and not birdsong, a single whippoorwill
whistling beneath the window.

Anaphylaxis

I wipe my hand across death's edge—

           for me,
           a dozen suns burning in a
              stand of Russian sage
           beside the barn. Black and
             yellow. Black and red.

      Drunk on pollen, their barbs lick at fear
                this far into summer's end.

And how many days do *we* shuffle mere inches from the grave?
I brush my hands through lavender leaves to feel the buzz

        against my knuckles like rings on a consecrated priest.
        The last time—a kiss just beneath the knee—

                the nurses looked like they
                  could see my soul

      leaving my body. As in a cartoon, some webby echo
        lifting from the bed.

Today I'm spared, only orbited

      in the backyard by a cloud of gold,
      fuzzy spheres harvesting what's left of the season. Burning

        wood and downed leaves and sap of dying aspens.

      But for just a moment, I lifted the lid on that other world,
      and my brain hummed a dirge for my body,
           and I stepped inside a perfect question.

Deadheading

Pills gleam like moons on the kitchen table,
but instead I turn to trimming,

raze burnt beds of sedum and cut
the drooping coreopsis.

At the yard's edge, I hold the dead
and unruly. Velvet flames sprout from my hands.

The earth takes everything back.
Perhaps my body will follow yours to the same,

same dust, same florid firing bush.
Or maybe this is just the world

turning its shoulder away again.

A Prayer for Mysticism

Let a bright and inexplicable bulb burn in my periphery like a lighthouse broadcasting calm waters.

Let stones and trinkets glitter my path, line the corners of my bedroom like monks or wardens.

The monkshood bowing at the river's edge, let them lift their pearl heads as in revelation.

Let the dead—my ancestors, my brothers—call from the bells in the churchyard, from the needle scratch at the back of every café I enter.

The fires on my bedstand—chirping disasters in my pocket—may they extinguish like matches in a wet book.

Let this trail of fear turn to ash or stars, a snow-white veil falling on my shoulders.

Let wild animals follow behind me like I've innards stuffed in my pockets, my pockets brimming with bloody meat.

Let the rancid runoff of a life lived turn treat for a wolf or bear or fox who stalks me and says my name over and over, sings me blessings in a dozen languages, and cleans me like a saucer, cleans me like a child, laps at my face then blinks its golden eyes to disappear.

Nuns in the Record Room

Graceland

Past the electric hum of the jungle room,
past the velvet curtains turned down
and the whispers of the lonely baby grand,
a bevy of nuns pace the mirrored halls.
In silence, in earphones, one habited head
hangs back, reflected above a pastel suit
and shoes, suede and tassels resurrected
in the reverent glow of the record room.
She lifts a sweaty hand to the case, holds
her robes to press a palm against the glass.
What prayers come to her here, kneeling
at the altar of a false God? What does she make
of the audio guide's earnest sermon?
A roar of footage from the racquetball room
calls her on. *The end of the tour*, they say
and try not to mark the euphemism—
all our lives reduced to objects, to a slow act
of accumulation. But in the gift shop,
a song loops as though it will never end,
as if it has been playing since the Beginning,
and behind us, the studded suit stands up
as if never taken off, alive and thrusting,
and a smudge of her hand hangs on the glass,
a shadow dancing just above his hips.

A Herd of Marbled Cows on a Hill in Kentucky

A herd of marbled cows grazes
on a hill in Kentucky, soaked in fog.

That's me there on the hill, a ceramic steer
perched above the rest.

I'm stoic, but alone, a spectacle, but also
a stone copy. On a hill in Kentucky,

a herd of marbled cows. Unhook your shirt
of fog, Kentucky. Lay bare your chest.

That pasture, marbled with cows, gives way
to another, the same. And another

version of me, this time a dinosaur,
rusted green, calling the weary off

the highway. In Kentucky the highway parts
the cliffs. I'm inanimate, unstuck from the world

of the living. Fog marbles the cliffs. The cows
stretch for miles. There I am. And there.

I'm so peripheral here. I'm made to hold
the eye, but not expected to speak or do much,

not expected to sing or write. I'm an effigy,
marbled in fog, waiting to ignite.

After Dinner, David Makes a List of Dead Friends

Candles behind the fake hydrangea
swamp the room in blood,
and a quiet game of *Clue* breaks loose,
morose, the weapons slightly off—
revolver or noose, pills, booze,
a trench of inescapable loneliness.
Don't you fucking dare, she says
in the car on the way home, though
my sadness has never taken
that particular form. Like a painting
in the passenger seat, she sits
stoic and transfixed. Her eyes
vibrate like sky-blue brushstrokes.
Outside, streetlights wobble
in the wind and drip blinking
game pieces—yellow, green, red—
onto the streets and sidewalks
and shoulders full of dirty snow,
and we drive on into the night,
our silence smothering the radio.

My Dead Friend, I Say, Though You Are Healthy and Well

No wake to mark this. No black cars or cigarettes
in the parking lot. No casseroles. No crows

at a graveside service. Instead, just a slippage—
your face less yours, your laugh muffled

like a river beneath an icy window. I can't stop seeing
headstones. I can't stop dreaming of that

day in Boston when we walked the Freedom Trail
in a spray of snow. *Cannon smoke*, you said,

a joke that flew off as we walked the crumpled tombs
at Copp's Hill, a metaphor we could not yet understand.

Tourists fumbled around us, miserable
student groups and couples huddled against the wind

and the unaccompanied, who walked with their arms
outstretched in the desperate gesture of the undead.

The Hemingway House

Key West

A glaring. A clowder.
>   Sixty or so six-toed cats
>   slink the grounds,

slip between
>   the hostas and fig
>   trees like ghosts

or vespers.
>   They leave behind
>   deviant prints,

galleys of oddity,
>   proof of the past
>   encased in mud.

Polydactyl, meaning many
>   fingers or, in prosody,
>   many feet—

one stressed syllable
>   followed by two unstressed.
>   Follow on your finger—

parable, trembling
>   *family,*
>   *shotgun shell.*

In the yard, the cats hunt
>   and spar. They raze
>   the caretakers' gardens.

Like grief, or the memory
                of grief, how it hangs
        around, skulks

and licks itself raw
                and leaves behind
        only a set of partial paws—

a twisted litho, reminder
                we all bend, at last,
        and return as echoes.

Look, Jeff, When You Get to California

Look, Jeff, when you get to California
don't go first thing to the surf.

Don't stand in the warm spray and wait
for dusk to drop a green eye

in the sea. Don't spend afternoons
loafing, feeding the belligerent

birds in Balboa Park or making faces
to penguins at the zoo. Like Seuss, you

will only find yourself more human.
Don't find that strip of narrow beach

south of the naval base where I buried
polished stones in a midnight ritual

I thought I didn't believe in. Sweet Anna.
Please don't find sweet Anna, lounging,

I'm sure, on her rooftop near the border,
still in her monkey flower dress.

Don't give her your love or even glance
in her direction. She will turn

it back on you like the tide
with a force that will make you

forever regret the broken stones
you were, fragile sand that you've become.

Storm King with John Ashbery

I was young and sad. I was meant to meet you
that fall on a trip to Storm King with Emily and Kevin
but then you died, and for days the sun refused
each time I stepped from my apartment building
to smoke or look for letters in the rusted bin.
In a dream, we walked the grounds in silent overcast.
We traced Calder's bloodlines, sat on wavy lawns
in fields of metal flowers. Kevin prayed since we had
nothing else left to say for you as eulogy.
I said he should pray in puns, elliptical directives
or pop culture allusions, but that wasn't as funny
out loud as it had been in my head. There was
no more language in the world, no more singing.
There, in the world, was the language for everything.

Full Moon

As if a glass dome
grows in my gut—

fishbowl or cloche.
Might call the feeling

soulless or *vacant*,
a bucket pulled up

from the well
holding only dust.

But it's spooky
season here,

so I'm searching
the streets—

rutted pumpkins
and headless

horsemen haunting
hawthorn trees—

I'm searching
the neighborhoods

for ghosts. Give me
swirling mist.

Give me chains
scraping sidewalk,

buckle glint
of an undead soldier.

Dusty rags. Blood-
stuck stomach.

Give me fiddle
song, down-tuned

by bones used
in the pegs

and fretboard—
a woman's bones,

no doubt, or a child's.
Give me children

in white robes
floating dewy lawns,

marking doorways
with whispers.

Give me the vicious
black dog

unlocked
by moonlight

that hunts dusk
at the edge of town.

Give me even
his teeth

or a trail of blood
running back

beneath the overpass.
A single breath

along my neck,
goosebumps,

a weighted sternum.
Belief is like skin—

we shed it
until we die

and then it's eaten
and dispersed again

to the newly living.
Give me the dead

tonight, troves
of them

clambering
up from the dirt,

some sign
I'm not alone,

some sign
another story

still waits in the dark.

The Emily Dickinson House

I didn't know, that summer,
a sparrow on the path could write
the world, death could

drive me home. I was young
and so lost to these hymns.
The tour guide showed us

Emily's desk and study, her
single bed, and you both laughed
at something I thought I'd missed

from the poems. At dusk,
on the way home, mile markers
slipped like pearls on a string,

rows of too-green trees
reminding me I was still lonely
and still in New England.

And when you asked to be
dropped off together,
I tried not to look wounded

or surprised, your naked bodies
tangling in my mind as you walked
arm in arm down the drive.

The world is full of dark
horses, emerging suddenly
from a darker sky. *I'm nobody,*

who are you? I said to the rearview
and thought what else
I didn't know about my life.

Memory

We wait for the right metaphor—

        box kite, creek bed,
petals dropped along the sidewalk.

But time waits for no one, they say.
Time plows each of us over.

I stood inside her doorway, half drunk
but mostly in love,

        as she pressed petals beneath wax paper.

Myositis—forget-me-nots, mouse ears,
blue stars pinned in a constellation on the table.

Her left side hung shrunk
and twisted from an accident she'd mentioned

but that I'd been unable
to ask about again. Such a coward—

I was already leaving,
already hooked by habit, by fear's loose springe.

Already leaving when she took my hand
and ran it down the crooked branch of her arm.

        Already leaving when she said, *please stay*.

Outside on the walk, a trail of petals
bent on into the night

like a rosary laid out by the wind . . .

Give us this . . .

at the hour of our death . . .

the resurrection of the body . . .

Amen.

Adornments

Coming down off a fist of mushrooms, I bent to double a lace, and when I stood, the horizon vanished, eaten by a mob of grazing mule deer. The biggest wore a thick shag, one errant antler as if to mock my mind's altered state. In my time here in the West, I've learned to call canyons canyons, and valleys valleys, learned too how the ugly deer here shed their antlers in spring, break in graceful rows across the rock face. On the ridge that day, a pack cut perfect lines, as if to split the sky, my brain turning the clay and silt striations like scarves around their ruddy heads. All horned beasts are chemically dependent, I've learned since, their adornments tied to doses wedged in at hot spots beneath the skull. Even now, in a lab somewhere, a mischief of mice spills from its cage, each beast sporting its own set of horns, each beast searching the world for answers.

From Someone's Tent Across the Field,
an iPhone Alarm Clock Won't Stop Singing

Over the river's edge,
through purple sage
and cattails padding
like a drummer's mallets,
the tone kicks and kicks
and keeps on kicking.
The song is a rudder,
rips us up from under
sleep's moldy hull.
We're holding tight
to last night's pretense
—tents in the woods
beside bending water,
music and stocked
coolers and plates
of powdered starlight.
But someone forgot
to kill the power.
The melody walks
along the ridge—
through smoke weed
and pillows of yarrow—
and shakes away
the home we built
here, erases the story
we've told ourselves.
The chirping stops
and starts again
like a bony hand
playing black keys
on the wind.

Search Party

Last night, by firelight, our laughter twisted us
             nearly to flames. When we yelled at the sky,

                          coyotes yelled back. Stars too, their voices
like pinched drops of moonlight.

                 But this morning, embers shrivel in the ring,
                          a sickness rising on coils of smoke.

Someone's gone missing—our headcount broke—
             and over camp-toast, we count

                          the landscape's deadly possibilities. The river,
a casket. The ridge that once caught sunset

                 like a dividing crystal, dotted now with rot
                          and fire kill, beetles rooting felled pines

like frostbit fingers. We all exhale together
             when Lucas finally emerges on the ridge, shirtless

                          and sunburnt and unharmed. He drags
behind a stag's leg, severed at the knee

                 and picked clean. The dogs circle at a distance, sniffing
                          recent death, and we each give thanks,

beneath our breath, for life and for living it
             with brilliant abandon.

Day Moon

On the trail today a day moon's thumb
watches us weave and climb.

                    A cairn. A blazon. Our directions
pulled on its icy string.

And I know as soon as I see it, that she will stop and shake her fist,
a joke about it existing in the wrong time and place—

     You dumb moon, I mouth, and then she stops
and says the same. Her beautiful mind doubling
         down on a joke

long held between us. A simple symptom of staying in love—
         a moon joke repeated in my head and then on her tongue,

and after, only the sound of our breathing, our minds
singing rounds beneath the golden aspens.

About the Bent Birch I Was So Sure Was a Bear

Famished, furious, the spring run batters
      the limestone, blows over

the great boulders. Grey-green as a waving
      wizard's beard. *Next to the throne*

of heaven—some bit I've stolen from
      Harrison and stowed

these years like a drunken bird;
      let this be the prayer to

brighten my nest. Let this, or this.
      This mineral throne perched

above the river, passerines
      sucking morning air,

chanting the news, their slight warnings.
      They know so much better

than me about the world. About the bent birch
      I was so sure was a bear

I howled and then waited out my echo
      for the silence again.

This, the fear we were designed for.
      A higher order than the others.

That our parents are dying, or my friend
      living so much he is

lost to me now. Or the whole world
      behind me shriveling

in its coat of plastic, in the toxic
          sun. When I'm done

coming here to be humbled, I will slip
          in the raging waters and rest.

A casket of river or a casket of mold.
          A eulogy folded out

on the palms of brilliant anemones
          as they spike and bloom

and die again. The water singing on
          and singing on and singing . . .

Nowhere to Run

Today is a fine day at dawn.
A great green settles here, the weight
of the air, each strand of each thing
moving of its own accord.
Even the leaves are audible, some subtle
croon settled down here in the valley.
On Main Street, the fans in the lofts
spin in the slow wind—propellers
turning the memory of industry.
Maybe the best day I ever lived
was that day in Detroit
when I danced with Martha Reeves
to "Dancing in the Streets,"
even if we weren't really *in the streets*
but at a union rally, a musty canopy
hung like a wet net above our heads.
A dozen of us shook and thanked God
and Lake Erie for the rain and for sweat
and for touching hands to waists.
There are hundreds of bad stories
hung like masks on the buildings
across this country, hundreds of places
left behind, but in this quiet valley,
narrow streets tilted like a bowl
full of hallways, mountains like
steeples or a row of distant crowns,
thousands of miles and a dozen years
from Wayne County, I hold out
as the day opens for the slow sound
of rain over the ridge, the rage
of the quarry to build into a soft chorus
of "Come and Get These Memories,"

or that last cold coda from "Nowhere to Run."
Time, try to take from me a place
I once knew well, and I will hold it
like an old song inside the foundations
of this town. I will tuck its edges
beneath these skinny streets
and shout all the truths I know
into every open space I see.

Poems for Detroit

If Philip Levine wrote acrostics,
he would always start with "lunchbox."
A "late shift ending" perhaps, before an
"under the small sparks of heaven."

If Robert Hayden, maybe the word
would be "nightmare," or maybe "daydream."

In the second-grade class today, the usual buzzing.
My students hide their neighborhoods
inside small animals and insects:
"this is a fine city / but I hate / bees."

And the teacher aides hand bits of praise
as though they were writing their own poems.
Just for being here, they said, *for directing
a dozen tiny symphonies in the classroom.*

My colleague sees in Charlie a prodigy.
Who's got the heart to tell him
those are Drake lyrics
and that it means, probably, that he is?

The page opens for some of them
like a life vest, for others, like a butterfly
knife, Phillips-head, and corkscrew.

When my own poems get mixed in—
a printing error—with a stanza
of "The Negro Speaks of Rivers,"
my shame is endless and the absurdity
of this shame, endless.

Were poetry like counting, I would
do it on my fingers.
Were teaching, I would let go
of numbers for good.

And can we say aloud now how unlike
living it is to write a poem?
Give me one letter and then another
and another and let us fill in the rest in unison.

Lucille Clifton's Baltimore

a vinyl sky
turns over
and over

a crow chews
wet trash
to wet froth

the Inner Harbor
washes out
like a blank page

row houses
like stanzas
like slant rhymes

thank God for this
the semicolon
the short line

that knowledge
and self-
knowledge grow

like two branches
on a tree
thank God

I stretched
and broke and budded
like a tree

and was tended
along the way
that the tender

set down
your language
in front of me

when I was young
that your language
fixed my roots

outside myself
I am only now
exhuming

the bad soil
old and poisoned
I am only now

beginning to see
the rotten timberland
I came up in

there are curves
in the brain that
like a dead stump

must be ground out
flattened by force
force of language

force of song
you still sing here
I'm still listening

Love Poem Written at Mina Loy's Grave

"Immortality mildews . . . in the museums of the moon."

—Mina Loy

My bones won't know
when your bones are

placed beside them or
that the fingers crumbling

in the adjacent grave
once fit like keys

inside my crooked teeth
or that even near the end

your skeleton walked
two inches taller than mine

your nose bone leaning in
over the dinner table

at night to gently nudge
my skull plate.

Leap Year

My friend John has no birthday
most of the time. He doesn't know
when to celebrate his own life.
Behind the register, at the bookstore,
we sneak news and baseball scores
from ancient computer monitors.
Money folds like paper flowers
back and forth across the counter.
We take turns, in shifts, trying to quit
smoking. John talks about Desire
and then Oblivion. *Thirty is the decade
of the body*, he says—*time is a key
turning its teeth through your muscle,
through your brain*. Like the cat
and mouse cartoon. The one
with the invisible ink, some force
to take your limbs from you
and then your body and then
your mind. There's another one,
YouTube tells me, but this one's
a duck with some vanishing cream.
The duck acts as an accomplice
to the mouse in his desire to slip
through the dirty seams of this world.
Once they take the plunge, they drop
from sight completely, knowable only
by the objects they disturb together,
the disorder they leave in their wake.

After Hours at the Last Word

A horn tips its golden bucket,
                            valves pressed down
            then limp like tongues.

The second solo turns
                            staccato on the bassline,
            runs a rowdy comeback.

The spotlights stammer
                            an echo, chasing down
            the calfskin, its shuffle—

dead stars, a bouquet
                            in each brushstroke.
            And beneath,

the cymbal shimmers.
                            On downbeats, the drummer
            tosses a clutch of coins

there on the high hat
                            as if to say *go ahead, count them.*
            So pocket, says the barback,

worked and sweating.
                            Like life, says the tender,
            cutting limes to quarters.

We are all looking
                            for a response,
            something earnest

but improvised. At last call
                            we are all swinging
            wild around the root.

ACKNOWLEDGMENTS

Many thanks to the editors of the following publications, where earlier versions of these poems first appeared:

Arkansas Review: "Nuns in the Record Room"
Autofocus: "My Father's Breathing"
HAD: "Junk" and "Shadow Ball Haibun"
Hunger Mountain: "Memory" and "After Dinner, David Makes a List of Dead Friends"
The Literary Review: "Irregular Heartbeats at the Park West" and "A Herd of Marbled Cows on a Hill in Kentucky"
New Mexico Review: "The Emily Dickinson House"
Nimrod: "The Fiberglass Man"
Rattle: "Relic"
Southeast Review: "Poems for Detroit"
Southern Indiana Review: "Stop-Motion with Sunken Carcass"
Two Peach: "Pyromaniac"
Yes Poetry: "Flight Plans"

The poems "Full Moon" and "Day Moon" first appeared in the chapbook *Our Natural Satellite*, published by Harvard Square Press.
"Nowhere to Run" first appeared in *Language Lessons: Volume 1*, published by Third Man Books.

*   *   *

"The Emily Dickinson House" borrows a line from Emily Dickinson.
"James Tate's Bookshelf" borrows a line from James Tate.
The quoted line in "Day Moon" is by Buzz Aldrin, from his appearance on *30 Rock*.

*   *   *

Thank you to those who encouraged me in this project over the years, especially Aaron Burch and Matt Kirkpatrick, Ben Fidler, David J. Daniels, Chet Weise, and Franke Varca. Thank you to Bianca Stone for her invaluable insights on an earlier version of this manuscript.

Thank you to the mentors, colleagues, and friends who continue to make me a better person and a better artist: Keith Taylor, Robert Fanning, Laura Kasischke, Raymond McDaniel, Joe Horton, Brad Benz, Chris McCormick, Mairead Small Staid, Josh Edwards, the winter/sessions boys, and the Camp Greensky crew. Special thanks to Michael Delp for his boundless wisdom and guidance.

Thank you to my parents for their love and support and to my brother John, who shares so much creative energy and inspiration.

And finally, deep gratitude to Aubrey. Thanks for loving my weird poet-brain and for choosing to share a life with me. And thanks, of course, for bringing home Freddie and Oso.

ABOUT THE AUTHOR

RUSSELL BRAKEFIELD is an assistant professor in the University Writing Program at the University of Denver. He is the author of *Field Recordings* (Wayne State University Press) and a graduate of the University of Michigan's Helen Zell Writers' Program. His poems have been published in over thirty literary magazines, and he has been awarded fellowships from the University Musical Society, the Vermont Studio Center, and the National Park Service.

Enjoy this sample
from Russell Brakefield's poetry collection

Field Recordings

Firmly rooted in the dramatic landscapes and histories of Michigan,
Field Recordings uses American folk music as a lens to investigate themes of
personal origin, family, art, and masculinity. The speakers of these poems
navigate Michigan's folklore and folkways while exploring more personal
connections to those landscapes and examining the timeless questions that
occupy those songs and stories. With rich musicality and lyric precision, the
poems in *Field Recordings* look squarely at what it means to be a son,
a brother, an artist, a person.

Order from your local bookstore, bookshop.org,
or from wsupress.wayne.edu

Mackinac Island

"It is no more possible to predicate the conduct
of an Indian than that of a woman."
~folklorist Charles M. Skinner in 1896

In the picture, my younger brother hangs slack
from the stocks, his hands wrung by wooden shackles
like he were made for that time— unlikely colonial cap
tilted up on his tiny, hinged-in head. The island flattened
to a dream-map for us then. Fudge and high walls. Cap guns
hung like meat from the shop stalls. And just beyond,
my mother's hand cuts sun from her eyes, my father
behind the lens. Not content to live among a crate of plastic
bows and arrows—the swaying commerce of violence—
she has been made villain by her objection, made more foreign
to our little boyhearts. In another photo, in a schoolroom
diorama, she leans against a roll-top desk, shadowed
by the under-lit fort. I stand before her with a mock musket,
peering wildly down the barrel at my would-be savage captor.
The pitch from the log wall has stained her neck and hair.
She splays her digits out across a desk's surface, capsized
by silence, and traces scars cut deep into the dreamwood.

Northern Michigan After Bar

Scrape of cotton to dirt and somewhere far off
the high bawl of pups, as we dip from our clothes
into the naked air and edge toward the lakeshore
where two black trays wobble against one another.

The group splits apart into disparate clusters,
buoys held waist-deep and limbed together.

I walk out on the water—a little Poseidon
with bad vision—and turn a wake into the darkness.
The others make their own small storms behind,
the shape of the night shrinking down around us.

Nain Rouge, Red Gnome

The gnome came to him in a dream,
passed on as omen
in the bruise-blue pall of sleep.

Like all gnomes—a neologism,
a wrong fold of the tongue.
The game telephone, I'm told, is false
whispers elsewhere.

Awake, he was a man changed,
his ambition ripened
by the courage of facing small
and foreign gods.

So the name bloomed new fear—
Nain Rouge, Red Gnome—
and roamed like a song as it had before.

From the Cree and Ojibwa—
a man made of speech alone.
And so not unlike myself.

So you want the tongue of god, I read
again and again
in my college dorm room,
not to be godlike, but to exist.